explaining
EPILEPSY

LIONEL BENDER

A⁺
Smart Apple Media

Smart Apple Media
P.O. Box 3263, Mankato, Minnesota 56002

Printed in the United States of America at
Corporate Graphics in North Mankato, Minnesota.

Published by arrangement with the Watts
Publishing Group Ltd, London.

Library of Congress Cataloging-in-Publication Data
Bender, Lionel.
  Explaining epilepsy / Lionel Bender.
      p. cm. – (Explaining–)
  Includes index.
  ISBN 978-1-59920-309-6 (hardcover)
  1. Epilepsy–Juvenile literature. I. Title.
  RC372.2.B46 2010
  616.8'53–dc22
                              2008049292

Planning and production by Discovery Books
Limited
Managing Editor: Laura Durman
Editor: Gianna Williams
Designer: Keith Williams
Picture research: Rachel Tisdale

Photo acknowledgements: Getty Images: pp. 11 (Nick Veasey),
16 (Pedro Ugarte/AFP), 23 (Stockbyte), 28 (Gary Buss),
36 (Time & Life Pictures); www.HopeForSydney.com: p. 39;
istockphoto.com: pp. 14 (Bradley L. Marlow), 19 (Nemanja
Glumac), 20 (Dr. Heinz Linke), 25, 27 (Zilli), 31 (Willie B.
Thomas), 35 (Gabriel Moisa); www.JohnBirdsall.co.uk: front
cover top, front cover bottom left, pp. 9, 13, 18, 30, 33, 34,
37; Science Photo Library: front cover bottom right (Josh Sher),
pp. 21 (AJ Photo Hop American), 24 (Mark Thomas)

Source credits: We would like to thank the following for their
contribution: Dr. Donald Weaver for Stephen and Colin's stories.

*Please note the case studies in this book are either true life
stories or based on true life stories.*

*The pictures in the book feature a mixture of adults
and children with and without epilepsy. Some of the
photographs feature models, and it should not be implied
that they have epilepsy.*

9 8 7 6 5 4 3 2
32010
1205

Contents

8 What is Epilepsy?

10 Causes and Effects

12 Who has Epilepsy?

14 Partial Seizures

16 Generalized Seizures

18 Triggers

20 Diagnosis

22 How You Can Help

24 Controlling Epilepsy

26 Taking Medicines

28 Living with Epilepsy

30 Epilepsy and Families

32 Epilepsy at School

34 Sports and Leisure

36 Growing Up with Epilepsy

38 Epilepsy Treatments

40 Glossary

42 Further Information

44 Index

What is Epilepsy?

Epilepsy is a condition of the brain. It is caused by a fault in the brain's communication system. The basic symptom of epilepsy is called a seizure and is a sudden short event where there is a change in a person's awareness, movement, or behavior. During an epileptic seizure, people may be unsure of where they are, what they are doing, their behavior, or their feelings. Sometimes people lose consciousness, may fall over, and start to shake uncontrollably.

A Condition

Epilepsy is a condition. It is not a disease that can be caught from another person. Over 3 million Americans are affected by epilepsy. Epilepsy affects people of all ages, but is most common in children and the elderly. During infancy, a child's brain is growing and developing, and it is at this stage that problems can occur that cause epilepsy to develop later. However, epilepsy can also be caused by accidents that involve blows to the head, or by brain tumors.

HIPPOCRATES MAKES THE LINK

A Greek doctor, Hippocrates (460–370 B.C.), was the first person to make the link between epilepsy and the brain. Hippocrates is often called "the father of medicine" because he was the first to understand many of the principles of health and diseases. Today, doctors often sign a modern version of the Hippocratic Oath, a summary of his beliefs, to show their commitment to do the best for their patients.

Definitions

The word "epilepsy" comes from the Greek word "epilambanein," meaning to "seize," or "take hold of." A person with a particular type of severe epilepsy can have a seizure that is also known as a fit, a convulsion, an attack, or a blackout. The term "epileptic" is sometimes used to describe a person with epilepsy, but really it should be used only to describe situations arising from the condition, such as an "epileptic seizure," or in medicines such as "anti-epileptic" drugs.

The Signs of Epilepsy

How epilepsy affects people varies. It is often hard for a person with epilepsy to say whether his or her symptoms are mild or severe. Certain kinds of seizures can go undetected, and around half of people with epilepsy do not experience seizures at all.

Epilepsy affects people all over the world. Most people with epilepsy can lead normal lives if their seizures are controlled, and some of them grow out of the condition as they get older.

▲ *People of all ages and races may be affected by epilepsy and have no outward signs of the condition, apart from seizures.*

Causes and Effects

The brain works like a computer. It is the body's control center and is made up of millions of microscopic interconnecting neurons, or nerve cells. Messages pass to, from, and within the brain as electrical signals through the neurons. A person with epilepsy can experience a temporary disruption or overload of neuron messages.

The Nervous System

Neurons are made of a cell body containing the nucleus, which is the cell's own control center, and a nerve fiber called the axon. The outer part of the brain, known as "gray matter," is made up mainly of the cell bodies of the neurons. The inner part of the brain is "white matter," which is made up of the nerve fibers leading from the neuron cell bodies.

Some of these fibers are short and interconnect with neurons within the brain. Other fibers are more than a meter in length and run down the spinal cord to muscles in the chest, legs, and arms. A special group of long fibers, forming the vagus nerve, carries signals to and from the brain, down through the neck, to the digestive system and heart. The brain, spinal cord, nerve fibers, and special neurons within muscles and sense organs make up your nervous system.

Synapses

Neurons are packed close together, but do not actually touch each other. There are narrow gaps in between, called synapses. Neurons pass messages to each other across the synapses. Normally, the messages flow in an orderly direction, at regular speed and at a standard strength. In a person with epilepsy, messages become disturbed and disorganized and these changes can cause a seizure.

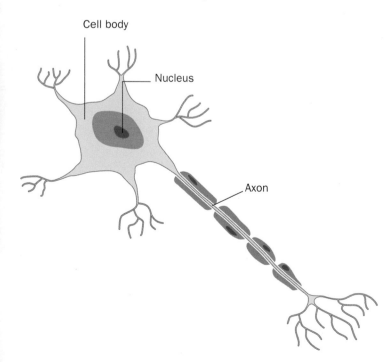

Cell body

Nucleus

Axon

◀ *A neuron is made up of a cell body and a long nerve fiber called an axon.*

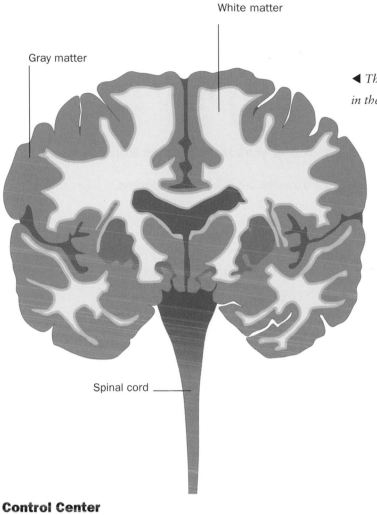

White matter

Gray matter

Spinal cord

◄ *The distribution of gray matter and white matter in the brain.*

Control Center

Different areas of the brain control different activities in the body. For example, there are areas for speech, memory, muscle action, consciousness, and body temperature regulation. Activities such as the beating of your heart, the digestion of food, and breathing are all automatic—they happen without any conscious effort. Your senses—including sight, hearing, taste, touch, and balance—also work automatically. Other activities, such as walking, switching on a light, or playing on a computer, require conscious effort: you think about doing these activities. For a person with epilepsy, the part of the brain affected by seizures can upset one or more of these activity centers and the actions related to them.

Different Types of Seizures

Epileptic seizures are divided into two main groups: partial and generalized. Partial seizures begin in one area of the brain and sometimes spread to other areas. There are three types of partial seizures: simple, complex, and secondarily generalized.

Generalized seizures affect the whole brain and they cause a person to lose consciousness. There are five types of generalized seizures: absence, myoclonic, tonic, tonic-clonic, and atonic. Absence seizures used to be called "petit mal" and tonic-clonic seizures "grand mal" from the French words meaning "small illness" and "great illness."

Some doctors regard all these terms as too general, because there is a whole spectrum of types of seizures with a wide variety of symptoms.

Causes

Scientists are still not sure exactly what causes problems in the brain's electrical system, or why it happens repeatedly in some people and not in others. About two-thirds of people with epilepsy have no visible physical difference in their brain.

Who has Epilepsy?

Epilepsy sometimes runs in families, which means that it may be an inherited condition. How your body looks and works is determined by your genes.

Genes and DNA

Genes are made up of strands of genetic material called DNA. DNA, which is found inside almost every cell in the body, contains all the information that is passed on from parent to child, such as eye color, hair color, and nose shape. DNA also contains a code that controls the production of proteins in the body. Proteins are involved in all chemical processes in the body. Sometimes genes do not work properly, or get damaged, or changed. It may be that epilepsy is caused by these genes.

Inheriting Epilepsy

Brothers and sisters, including non-identical twins, share many, but not all, of their genes. It is for this reason that only a small percentage of the siblings of people with epilepsy are likely to experience any kind of seizure in their lifetime. Identical twins have exactly the same genes as each other (see box), so you would expect that if one twin had epilepsy, the other twin would too. This is not always the case.

In one major study of children with epilepsy held in Melbourne, Australia, in the late 1990s, scientists found that in 20 percent of non-identical twins, both children had epilepsy. In identical twins, this figure went up to 65 percent. In the identical twins, the type of epilepsy they both had was almost always the same, making scientists strongly suspect that epilepsy is inherited.

Inheritance of one or more faulty genes can make some people susceptible to epilepsy, but even then, most of these people never experience any symptoms.

GENETIC MAKEUP

Genes (including those that could cause epilepsy) are passed from one generation to another during sexual reproduction. When an egg from a woman is fertilized by a sperm from a man, the genes of the egg and sperm are combined. Identical twins are the product of one fertilized egg that divides in two, hence the babies that develop have identical genes: the babies are of the same sex, and share the same blood group and same eye color. Non-identical twins are the product of two separate eggs and two separate sperm. The babies that grow from them have similar, but not identical, genes: the babies may be of different sexes, they may look different and they may have different blood types.

▲ *Though epilepsy may be inherited, this does not mean that a relative of someone with epilepsy will necessarily have epilepsy too. Even an identical twin of someone with epilepsy may not have the condition.*

Triggers

There seem to be several factors that can set off, or trigger, a seizure, and these are different for each individual. The factors include a lack of sleep or an illness.

High-Temperature Seizures

Not all seizures are a result of epilepsy. Though one in 20 people have a seizure during their lifetimes, only one in 50 of those people will be diagnosed with epilepsy. This is because other conditions can

FAMOUS PEOPLE WITH EPILEPSY

The soldiers and statesmen Alexander the Great, Julius Caesar, and Napoleon Bonaparte are all believed to have had epilepsy. The Soviet leader Vladimir Lenin had epilepsy. The actor Danny Glover, the comedian Rik Mayall, and musicians Martin Kemp and Adam Horovitz also have epilepsy.

also cause seizures. One example of this is febrile convulsions. This happens when children have a very high temperature during an infection. As soon as the child's temperature drops, the seizure ends.

Partial Seizures

Partial seizures are seizures that begin in one part of the brain. People having seizures may suddenly become confused or hear odd sounds. They may start to tug at their clothes or get up and roam around the room.

▲ *A child who experiences a partial seizure may feel dizzy for several seconds. The difference between a simple partial seizure and a generalized seizure is that a person does not lose consciousness during a simple partial seizure.*

There are three main types of partial seizure. With many parts of the brain potentially being affected, the symptoms of these seizures are many and varied. Some people have partial seizures with few outward signs so onlookers may not even realize the person is having a seizure.

Simple Partial Seizures

During a simple partial seizure, a person remains conscious and can remember what happens. Simple partial seizures are not necessarily unpleasant experiences. For example, some partial seizures cause only small movements, for example they may cause a person's finger to jerk. During other kinds of partial seizure, a person may smell or taste things that are not there, hear sounds, or feel numbness. A simple partial seizure may also cause someone to feel emotions like happiness or fear, for no obvious reason.

Auras

Sometimes a type of simple partial seizure, known as an aura, acts as a warning that the seizure is about to spread to the rest of the brain. Soon afterwards, the person may experience a generalized seizure (see pages 16–17).

Other Partial Seizures

If the seizure spreads to other parts of the brain, a person can experience two other kinds of partial seizures: complex partial seizures or secondarily generalized seizures.

In a complex partial seizure, a person may start to smack their lips, make chewing movements, or wander around looking confused. Many of these

people will tug at their clothing. These seizures can last a few minutes and the person may be tired or confused for a while afterwards.

Secondarily generalized seizures are partial seizures that spread to the rest of the brain and cause a person to lose consciousness and in some cases have convulsions.

Generalized Seizures

Generalized seizures are seizures that affect the whole brain from their onset.

They can happen at any time and a person who has one will lose consciousness.

Some people with epilepsy have frequent seizures, others rarely have them.

There are several types of generalized seizures. An atonic seizure is a kind of seizure where a person loses strength in his or her muscles.

A myoclonic seizure causes brief jerks of groups of muscles, often in the upper body. This kind of seizure often occurs just after a person wakes up.

▼ *If you see someone who has hurt themselves as a result of a seizure, you should call an ambulance and tell the medics exactly what you have seen.*

"When I fell over, my schoolfriends quickly moved all the desks and chairs away from me so I did not hurt myself. Afterwards I felt punch-drunk, like boxers must feel when they have been knocked out in the ring."

Tom, age 14, after a tonic-clonic seizure.

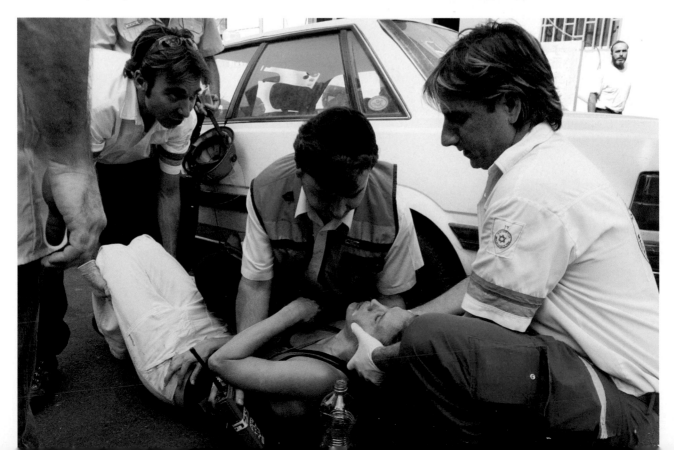

During an absence seizure, a person seems to be temporarily daydreaming or absent-minded. An absence seizure may last only a few seconds, but a person may experience hundreds in one day.

A tonic-clonic seizure is the most well-known generalized seizure. "Tonic" is a medical term for when muscles stiffen, and "clonic" describes when muscles contract and relax quickly in short bursts or spasms.

Stages of a Tonic-Clonic Seizure

If you see someone having this type of generalized seizure, you may notice this in the tonic stage:

1 The person may make a loud cry or scream. This is not from pain or fear, but the result of air being squeezed out quickly from the lungs as chest muscles contract. He or she loses consciousness, stiffens, and falls to the ground.

Then in the clonic stage:

2 Breathing may become noisy, or the person may seem to stop breathing and may become pale or start to turn blue.

3 The person's whole body starts to convulse (jerk or shake) rhythmically.

4 The person may wet themselves as they have no control over their muscles.

5 Finally, the person's muscles relax. The person usually regains consciousness at this time.

The After-Effects

Following a tonic-clonic seizure, people can feel drowsy and may have a headache and want to sleep. This can last for many hours. Because their muscles have been overworked and stretched, they may feel aches and pains for days after.

CASE NOTES

ANGELA'S STORY

Angela is 14 years old. When she was 8 years old she had meningitis, and soon after she experienced some tonic-clonic seizures. Then she was free from seizures for six years. After her fourteenth birthday she experienced her first serious tonic-clonic seizure at home. Her mother describes what happened:

"Angela was sitting on a chair in the kitchen having breakfast. Out of the blue she said she felt a little strange. Then she made a strange sound, like a grunt, and fell off the chair onto the ground. Luckily she didn't hit anything, but she did knock her bowl of cereal off the table and it crashed to the ground. Angela's body stiffened briefly, then started jerking. She seemed to stop breathing for a few seconds. This lasted several minutes. I didn't panic because I knew she was having a seizure. I made sure she would not bash against anything, but I did not touch her. Gradually her muscles relaxed and she became conscious."

Angela said afterwards: "I really don't remember very much about the seizure. I felt tired for a long time afterwards."

Triggers

Sometimes a situation or event triggers a seizure. It may be a flashing light, stress, or tiredness. Once a person with epilepsy has identified a trigger, he or she may be able to eliminate or reduce the number of seizures by avoiding situations that could bring on seizures. However, not everyone with epilepsy has a trigger.

Types of Triggers

Several situations can trigger a seizure. Some people with epilepsy have seizures during times of stress, or when they are tired, bored, or excited.

Light Sensitivity

Changes in light can be a trigger. About 3–5 percent of people with epilepsy are "photosensitive"—they are affected by the flickering or flashing of lights at a club or during a movie, or the flickering of a computer screen. Watching television is not usually a problem unless it is in a dimly lit or dark room. Taking a break from the screen every 30 minutes is a good idea. Some people with epilepsy find that wearing special photochromic glasses can reduce the effect of these triggers.

▼ *For some people with epilepsy, looking at certain types of computer screens can trigger a seizure.*

▲ *Bright flashing lights, such as the stroboscopic (strobe) lights at a concert or rave, can trigger a seizure in people with certain types of epilepsy.*

Fatigue

Tiredness caused by too many late nights, jet lag, or working night shifts can also act as a trigger for some people with epilepsy.

A Healthy Lifestyle

A healthy lifestyle is a good idea for everyone, not just people with epilepsy. Eating at least five servings of fruit and vegetables a day could help to fight infections that make some people susceptible to a seizure.

Thresholds

Each person has a threshold for seizures. If the threshold is low, the person is more likely to experience seizures. The threshold may also be affected by such activities as drinking alcohol, taking recreational drugs, or by hormonal imbalances in the body. All of these alter the activity of the brain and make a person more susceptible to any trigger. For example, one person's threshold for a seizure may be exceeded after only one alcoholic drink, whereas another person may be able to have several drinks before they are affected.

Diagnosis

A person who has had a seizure should be seen by a doctor to check for the cause. As a routine, premature babies or babies whose birth was difficult will be examined by a hospital doctor to check for any brain condition. Similarly, people who have injured their heads in an accident or suffered a serious brain infection, tumor or blood clot will be thoroughly examined to see if they are likely to develop seizures.

Building Up a Picture

Diagnosing epilepsy, identifying the causes, and finding the best course of treatment are all carried out by a neurologist. A neurologist is a doctor specializing in the functioning and condition of the body's nervous system, including the brain. The neurologist will ideally examine a patient while he or she is having a seizure, but this is unlikely to be possible. Instead, the doctor will ask family and friends to describe the frequency, symptoms, and after-effects of the patient's seizures.

Different Tests

Next, the neurologist may do a series of tests. First, he or she will try to find out if an illness could be the cause. This may involve doing a blood test to rule out other conditions, such as diabetes. Then the patient may have a test called an EEG, which records the pattern of electrical signals in the brain. Pads called electrodes are placed on the head, and they monitor how the brain reacts to possible triggers, such as flashing lights.

Scans

The neurologist may perform a scan of the brain to look for any possible causes of the seizure using an MRI scanner. This uses the movement of water in the brain to build up an image, which is then displayed on a computer screen.

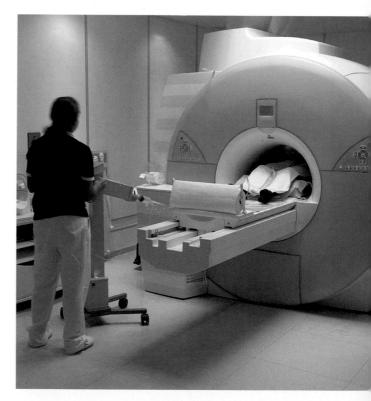

▶ *An MRI (Magnetic Resonance Imaging) scanner can be used to help diagnose epilepsy.*

KHAN'S STORY

Khan is 10 years old and is susceptible to absence seizures.

"To prepare for my EEG, the neurologist, Dr. Aziz, told me to have my breakfast early, at least two hours before my appointment at 10 a.m. I was not to have any fizzy drinks or snacks after that, and I should take my anti-epileptic medicine as normal. I should wash my hair in baby shampoo so that my scalp was free from any oils or perfumes. When I got to his office, the nurse put some gel at various places on my scalp and attached about 20 electrodes. Then the EEG began.

On one occasion, Dr. Aziz asked me to breathe rapidly and deeply for three minutes. This made me feel a little dizzy and tingly round the mouth. Then he asked me to close my eyes and he shone a flashing bright light in front of my eyes. The EEG lasted about an hour and did not hurt at all.

After my examination, Dr. Aziz showed me my EEG scan on the computer screen. He showed me a scan of a normal 10-year old boy and compared it to mine. I could see that in places the lines on my scan had more ups and downs."

▼ *An EEG measures the electrical activity of the brain by recording from electrodes, which are placed on the scalp.*

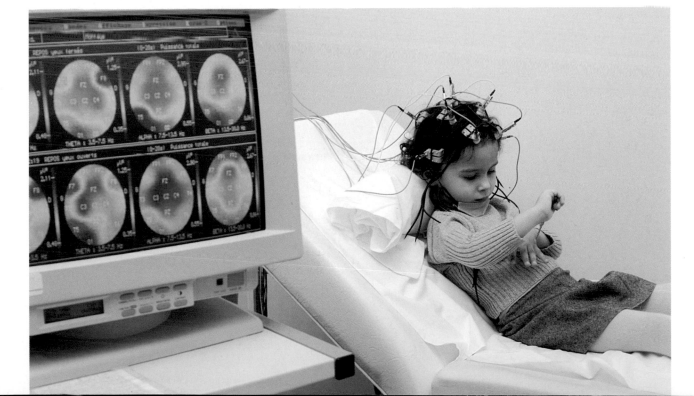

How You Can Help

The first time you see someone having a tonic-clonic seizure can be scary and unsettling. You cannot stop the seizure, but there are ways that you can help. The seizure will normally run its course in a few minutes. Staying calm will make you and any other onlookers feel more confident and reassured.

Dos and Don'ts

1 Do stay close to the person and keep calm.

2 Do move away any chairs, tables, or other objects that the person could bump into.

3 Do put something soft like a pillow or cushion under the person's head if they have fallen.

4 Do not try to move the person.

5 Do not put anything in the person's mouth.

6 When the seizure is over, do try to roll the person onto his or her side in the "recovery position" so that the airways are not blocked, and saliva can drain away.

7 Do talk to the person, telling them what has happened. The person may feel embarrassed, so try to reassure them.

8 If the person falls asleep afterwards, do regularly check if he or she is all right.

If the person having a seizure is someone you know and you are familiar with their symptoms, there is probably nothing more you need to do other than check they do not hurt themselves during the seizure. If it is a stranger and you are not sure of their condition, check for a medi-alert tag (see page 28) once the seizure is over. If you are still unsure, call for an ambulance. However, some people have several seizures a month and they may be upset if

▼ *Placing an unconscious person in the recovery position prevents their tongue from blocking their breathing and allows fluid to drain from their mouth. It is also a safe position to put someone in if you are forced to leave them alone.*

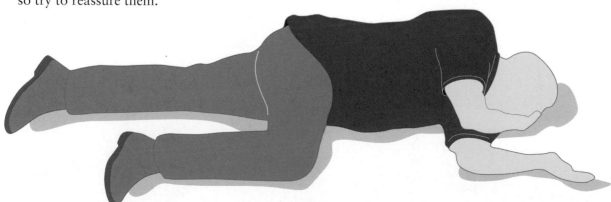

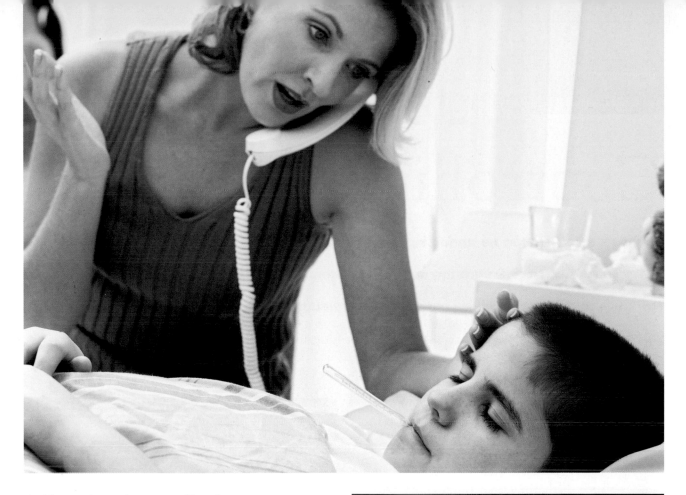

▲ *After a seizure, the person affected may want to rest. If it is the first time a child has experienced a seizure, a parent or caregiver should consult a doctor, who may recommend tests and a brain scan.*

they are taken to the hospital every time. If people do hurt themselves during a seizure, give them first aid only if you are trained to do so. You can harm an injured person by moving them in the wrong way.

Emergency Help

If you are unsure whether to call an ambulance, use the "two and five minute" rule. If you know the person, and the seizure lasts two minutes longer than is normal, then call an ambulance. If you do not know the person, or you don't know how long their seizures usually last, call an ambulance if the seizure lasts for five minutes. Keep a record of when the seizure started and what happened. This will help the emergency services and doctors.

TOM'S STORY

Tom experienced a tonic-clonic seizure when he was at a soccer game.

"My team had just scored and the next thing I remember was waking up near the touchline [sideline]. The St. John's Ambulance staff had brought me on a stretcher from the stands, where I had collapsed. Fortunately I was with my workmate, Derek, and he knew what to do. He waited till the seizure was over and then, just as a precaution, he called the ambulance. I was checked over and found to be fine. I stayed in the grounds till the match was over, then Derek took me home in a taxi. I slept all the way. At home I went straight to bed and felt fine in the morning."

Controlling Epilepsy

Because seizures can be upsetting, random, and can lead to injury, it is important to try to reduce their frequency or prevent them. In about 70 percent of people with epilepsy, drugs or medicines can do this. Avoiding the triggers that set off seizures will also help.

Drugs

Medicines used to prevent seizures are commonly known as anti-epileptic drugs (AEDs) or sometimes anti-convulsants. These work by reducing or eliminating the disruption of electrical signals in the brain, making the brain less susceptible to seizures. The medicines are taken regularly. As with any medicines, they can cause side effects, or unwanted reactions or feelings, such as skin rashes, sickness, or tiredness. Patients may need to try several drugs until the best one is found.

STATUS EPILEPTICUS

There is a very serious type of situation called "status epilepticus." A person may have a continuous seizure lasting more than 30 minutes or a series of seizures without gaining consciousness in between. In extreme circumstances, and if not treated quickly with medication, the condition can cause death. In the United States, there are more than 100,000 incidents a year of status epilepticus and about 20,000 of them result in death.

Surgery

For those people who do not respond to drugs, surgery may be an option and may be necessary in cases where epilepsy is caused by brain damage or a tumor. Surgery usually involves removing the part

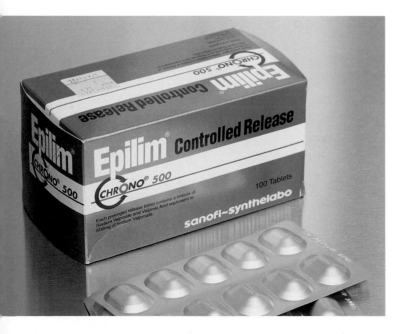

◀ *Epilin, a British anti-epileptic drug, reduces brain activity by increasing the amount of a chemical that blocks electrical messages passing from one neuron to another.*

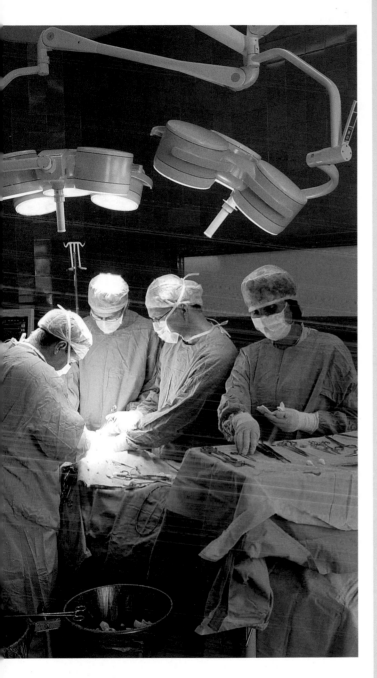

▲ *Brain surgery is a way of curing some forms of epilepsy, but it is a delicate operation and carries risks.*

of the brain responsible for the seizures. It is a very delicate operation as normal brain tissue must not be damaged—neurons cannot repair themselves.

RYAN'S STORY

Ryan had his first seizure when he was 32. An EEG helped show that his seizures were coming from a part of the left side of his brain. This had probably been caused 10 years earlier in a horse riding accident that left him unconscious for an hour. Over a period of five years, medication did not stop the seizures, so neurologists recommended surgery to remove the damaged part of his brain.

"The surgeon pointed out that there was only a 50 percent chance that removal of the damaged part of my brain would solve the problem. He also made it clear how serious the operation would be: there was a possibility of damage to the speech and memory centers of my brain, and that recovery would take several months. Before the operation, I had an EEG and an MRI scan and various tests to identify the exact location of the damaged part of my brain. During the operation I was occasionally woken up to check no damage had been done to healthy tissues."

After the operation, Ryan immediately became seizure-free, but after two years, the symptoms returned. He was put on new medication and has remained seizure-free for the last eight years.

Taking Medicines

As soon as a person is diagnosed with epilepsy, doctors may prescribe drugs to get the condition under control. Because drugs can affect many different cells in the body, the doctor will be careful about what dosage to prescribe. If the original dose is not effective, the amount will be increased a little at a time until the right level is found. The drug is taken regularly to build up and maintain the right level of the drug in the body.

Which Medicine?

With more than 40 different types of seizure, there are many types of AEDs, or anti-convulsants, that can be used. The drugs may be taken by mouth as pills or tablets. They are usually taken two or three times a day, for example, one dose after breakfast in the morning and one after dinner in the evening. Very young children may take their medicines as syrups.

It is important to take the drugs around the same time each day to maintain a constant level in the body. Some people store their pills in pill boxes. The boxes have see-through compartments for each day of the week to help remind them instantly whether or not they have taken the pills.

Like most medicines, AEDs can cause side effects in some people. For example, one type of AED has side effects that include tiredness, dizziness, blurred vision, skin rash, and excitability. These can in turn affect concentration and thinking. Side effects of other anti-convulsants can include hair loss, weight gain, and an abnormal heartbeat.

Complementary Treatments

Some people do not like taking medicines. They may try to find more natural, or complementary, forms of treatment, including acupuncture, homeopathy, and aromatherapy. None of these seem to be totally effective against epilepsy, but they may work alongside conventional medicines. Acupuncture involves using needles to stimulate the body's nervous system. Homeopathies try to stimulate the body's own defense systems with natural substances. In aromatherapy, a person is exposed to the smell of various natural oils. All of these treatments should only be used under guidance from a neurologist and a complementary treatment specialist.

CARE WITH MEDICINES

Many pills and tablets look like little candies, but if eaten by people who are not ill, or who have a condition other than epilepsy, they can be harmful. It is important that medicines are kept safely away from small children.

ROBERT'S STORY

Robert is 12 years old.

"I have to take my anti-epileptic drugs three times a day, but I am a little forgetful. My parents have bought me a watch with alarms set for 8 a.m., 2 p.m., and 8 p.m. to remind me to take my pills. During school terms, every Monday morning I give five pills to the head teacher, both for safekeeping and so that she can give me my afternoon pill each day. I keep my pills in a little box with a red cross and my name on it. At home my pillbox stays in my room. When I am out, I keep it in a little belt pouch and not in my pocket, where it may fall out. I have to make sure no other children can take my pills as they can harm someone who is not epileptic. My doctor and parents have told me that it is not serious if I miss a dose, and that everyone does this from time to time. However, this can cause some side effects so I should ask my teachers and friends to keep an eye on me when this happens."

▼ *Some people try to ease the effects of epilepsy with acupuncture. It is thought that by stimulating the body's nervous system with needles, electrical disturbances in the brain can be controlled or overcome.*

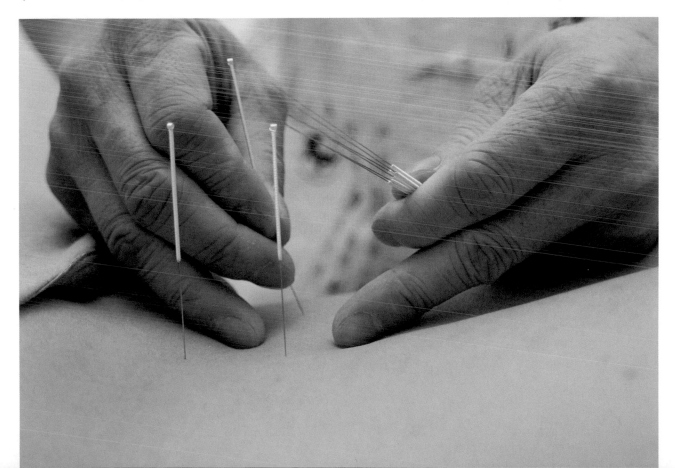

Living with Epilepsy

Most people with epilepsy lead normal lives if their seizures are controlled. If their medication works, they may never have another seizure. They can work most jobs and join in most sports and leisure activities.

Carrying an ID

To notify other people of their condition, many people with epilepsy wear a form of identification (ID), such as a medi-alert bracelet, wristband, tag, or necklace. Sometimes these carry information about their seizures and medication. Other people carry an ID card with this information on it.

Checkups

People with epilepsy may visit their doctor or neurologist every few months to update their history of seizures and to check that their medicine is still working well. At each visit, the doctor will check that the medication and dose are still appropriate.

Should a person grow out of epilepsy or be seizure-free for more than two years, he or she may decide together with the neurologist to stop taking medication. However, each person is different and the risks and benefits of taking the medicine, or not taking it, have to be weighed with the help of a neurologist. Taking any medicines when they are not needed is unnecessary and can be harmful.

Biofeedback

Some people with epilepsy are able to control their nervous activity to such a level that when they get an aura or unusual sensation, they can control their nerves so that a seizure does not happen. This is known as biofeedback. A person who uses biofeedback can control his or her body until it is able to regulate and correct itself naturally. To do this, a person with epilepsy has to learn how to interpret his or her EEG recordings and work out what to do to get any abnormal electrical activity in the brain under control. It requires a lot of testing, training, and practice. Biofeedback is a difficult skill to develop and so it is not used very often.

◀ *Medi-alert bracelets are a type of ID bracelet that look like jewelry, but contain important information about conditions such as epilepsy.*

Feeling Confident and Secure

Some people with epilepsy are worried about what will happen to them if they have a seizure. They are concerned how relatives, friends, and people at school or work may react. They might wish to explain to everyone they know what type of epilepsy they have, what might happen, and what other people should do if they need help. However, not all people with epilepsy will want to tell others about their conditions.

HOW BIOFEEDBACK WORKS

In biofeedback—also known as neurofeedback—a person with epilepsy works with a computer to monitor their brain wave patterns. EEG scans are taken of a patient's brain activity and shown to the patient on a computer. Patients concentrate on relaxation techniques and on breathing in the hope of changing their brain activity.

Other training sessions use videos where a patient watching a video of a fish is asked to concentrate on changing it into other shapes, such as a mermaid and then a star. If the patient's emotional state changes, then the shapes on the video screen also change.

Because of the sophisticated technology that is used during biofeedback training sessions, this type of treatment can be very expensive and it is not available in all countries.

Epilepsy and Families

For the parents, brothers, and sisters of someone with epilepsy, small adjustments can be made to make life easier. For example, their house might be made very safe from minor accidents.

Safety at Home

Just what safety features or practices would be helpful in the home depends on the type of seizure the person experiences and the things that trigger the seizure. Here are some examples:

1 Avoid furniture with sharp edges or cover the edges with foam or plastic.

2 Avoid letting the person sleep in a tall bunk bed in case he or she falls out during a seizure.

3 Encourage the person not to lock the bathroom door or take a bath or shower without telling someone else in the house. An "in use" sign on the door can help.

4 Have soft carpets on floors and stairs.

5 Watch TV in a well-lit room.

6 Fit safety glass to windows and doors.

7 Use back burners or hotplates on a stove and turn saucepan handles inward so they cannot be knocked down.

8 Use electronics that switch off automatically.

▶ *Watching TV in a well-lit room can reduce the chances of a seizure for those people who are sensitive to flickering light.*

Epilepsy Nurses

Some hospitals have special nurses who work with doctors and schools to give advice, information, and help to people with epilepsy and their families. Epilepsy nurses may visit homes to advise on safety, dealing with a seizure, and how to explain the condition to other people. They also give medical help and support to adults with epilepsy.

Family Vacations

People with epilepsy sometimes talk to their doctor or neurologist before going on vacation to get advice on any activities that could trigger a seizure. Traveling by car, train, or plane should not be a problem, but they should take food and drinks for the journey to ensure they can have regular meals. They should also take enough medicine for their stay. With long-distance travel that crosses international time zones, the schedule for taking medicine may need to be adjusted to suit local times.

PET PATIENTS

Cats and dogs can have epilepsy. The causes, effects, symptoms, and treatments of this condition in pets are very similar to human epilepsy. There are cases of pets experiencing a seizure when being taken to the vet, so it has been suggested that stress could be a cause.

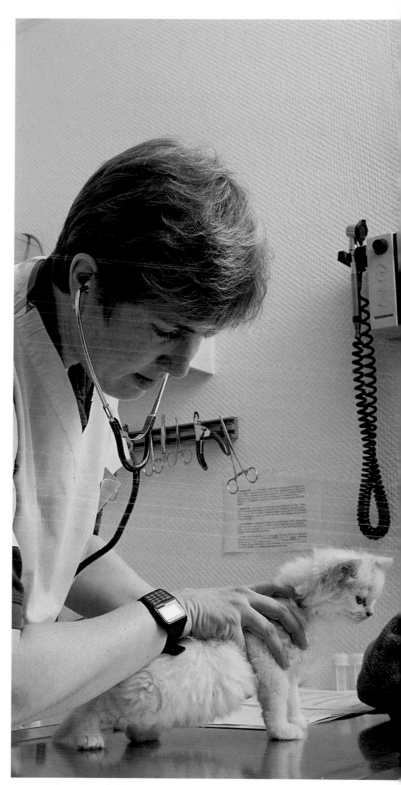

▶ *A pet with epilepsy requires similar attention and medication to a person with the condition. You should consult a vet if you think your pet may have had a seizure.*

Epilepsy At School

Most children with epilepsy attend mainstream schools and are able to join in all school activities. Teachers and students alike will benefit from learning about epilepsy and how to help a child who has the condition. However, not every school can provide the help and support needed, so some children will attend special learning centers.

Help Is At Hand

Any student that develops epilepsy may have to take days off school until his or her medication is figured out. The student may also find it difficult to concentrate in class and to do homework and exams. If they study for too long without a break, they can trigger a seizure. Epilepsy nurses may visit the school and help support the child when needed.

There are generally two main issues regarding epilepsy at school: the use of computers, and sports and outdoor activities. For those students likely to be affected by the flickering screens of computers, teachers should ensure the student works in a well-lit room and does not focus on the screen for too long at a time. For sports such as swimming, a student with epilepsy should be accompanied at all times in case help is needed.

School Trips

Going on a school trip requires preparation and support. Students with epilepsy must take along their medication and remember to keep to the strict timetable for taking it. Parents, teachers, and support staff can work together to ensure that the student can join in all the activities.

Learning Difficulties

Some students that have epilepsy as a result of brain damage at birth may find it difficult to learn at the same speed as other students. They may lack concentration or the ability to deal with lots of information and instructions. They may need special help with schoolwork. Many schools provide learning support teachers for this, and students work one-on-one with the teacher. Gradually, they may learn to read, write, and do math to high standards. Local epilepsy support groups often provide educational programs to help parents and teachers set up plans in schools.

Special Schools

Students who regularly have seizures and often lose consciousness may wear a helmet to protect their heads from injury should they fall down. This can make them feel uneasy in a mainstream school. There are schools set up to help students with special needs. The students may live at the school during the school year, and come home on weekends and holidays. At the school, teachers and helpers can make the students feel more confident.

▼ *Most students with epilepsy attend public schools. Some students with epilepsy will not have any problem learning, but others may need extra help.*

Sports and Leisure

Sports are a healthy and enjoyable activity for everyone, including people with epilepsy. The benefits of regular exercise usually outweigh the risks of a possible seizure. Most sports are suitable for people with epilepsy, sometimes with just a few extra safety precautions.

Doctor's Advice

It can be helpful for someone with epilepsy to discuss the possible dangers of an extreme sport with his or her neurologist or family doctor. Exercise is good for everyone and a person with epilepsy should keep active. However, he or she must take normal precautions, such as wearing a helmet for riding, bicycling, and other sports where a fall could result in a blow to the head.

Contact Sports

Contact sports need to be considered carefully by a person with epilepsy. For example, boxing should be avoided because a punch to the head could instantly cause a seizure. Football and hockey can be dangerous as well for those with a low seizure threshold. People who have epilepsy sometimes try out a particular sport for a short time at first. Then, if they have no adverse reactions, they can gradually build up the amount of time they participate.

▶ *Wearing a helmet when bicycling is a sensible safety precaution for everyone. For people with epilepsy, who may have a seizure when bicycling, it is essential.*

Gym Activities

Using a treadmill and other gym equipment is generally fine for people with epilepsy. Some people with epilepsy have to be careful not to "push themselves to the limit." If they use a sauna or jacuzzi, they must ensure they do not get too hot because this can trigger a seizure.

Extreme Sports

A person with epilepsy will have to carefully consider whether to take up extreme sports. Sports such as rock climbing may be dangerous for a person who experiences uncontrolled seizures. Scuba diving is considered dangerous for people who have seizures or are taking anti-epileptic drugs.

ALAN FANECA, PRO FOOTBALL PLAYER

Alan Faneca was diagnosed with epilepsy at the age of 15 and put on medication to control his seizures so he could continue to play football. Faneca has played in the NFL since 1998 and currently plays for the New York Jets. He has been a six-time Associated Press All-Pro choice (2001-02, '04, and '06-07).

▼ *Usually there is no reason why a person with epilepsy should not go to the gym to exercise.*

Growing Up with Epilepsy

**As a child's brain grows and fully develops, some forms of epilepsy may disappear.
Many people who have epilepsy as a child grow out of it in adulthood.**

Adult Life

In order to make sure that adults who have epilepsy stay safe and to ensure the safety of those around them, governments have introduced various guidelines. Adults with epilepsy may not be allowed to hold certain jobs where health and safety could be at risk. For example, there are legal restrictions on the types of jobs that people with epilepsy can hold in the armed forces. In the UK, local councils decide whether a person with epilepsy can drive a taxi. If a person with epilepsy has been free of

▼ *Lewis Carroll was the pen name of Charles Lutwidge Dodgson (1832–1898), a mathematician, photographer, and writer of children's books. His epilepsy influenced his work.*

IN WONDERLAND: THE STORY OF LEWIS CARROLL

As an adult, English author Lewis Carroll developed epilepsy and had severe headaches and migraines. Carroll recorded his seizures, and how they affected his writing, in his journals. In his diaries he used such terms and expressions as "fits," "eerie states" and "the waking dream." In his famous books, *Alice in Wonderland* and *Alice Through the Looking Glass*, Alice finds herself growing and shrinking, seeing objects larger, and smaller than reality, and falling down holes. It may be that these were Carroll's way of describing his seizures.

seizures for a year, he or she is allowed to drive a car. If a person only has seizures during their sleep for three years, he or she will also be allowed to drive a car.

Fighting Discrimination

The Americans with Disabilities Act ensures that a person who has a disability, such as epilepsy, must have the same conditions of employment as someone without the condition. Even someone who has had epilepsy in the past, but is no longer affected by it, is covered by the Act. An employer cannot use epilepsy as an excuse for not promoting someone, not giving them a pay raise or not paying them benefits.

▼ *People with epilepsy might use a panic alarm like this to get help if they hurt themselves during a seizure.*

Brain Damage

For a person who develops epilepsy as an adult, some adjustment to everyday life may need to be made. There is generally less support for adults than for children with the condition, and the side effects of medication may influence their lives differently. Often, epilepsy in adulthood develops as a result of a stroke or brain damage caused in an accident, but there are lots of possible causes.

In Later Life

Some people of retirement age naturally experience loss of memory, and those with epilepsy may find this gets worse as a side effect of their anti-epileptic drugs. This in turn may make them more likely to forget to take their medication regularly, which can make them more dependent on their alarms and helpers.

Epilepsy Treatments

There is constant research going on to try to treat epilepsy, but neurologists are not yet close to preventing or curing epilepsy completely. However, brain surgery is now possible without opening a person's skull, and anti-epileptic drugs are becoming more effective with fewer side effects.

Laser Surgery and Implants

Using the intense energy of a laser beam, surgeons can now cut away damaged parts of the brain or brain tumors without making major incisions. The beam can be accurately directed at a tiny part of the brain so that there is little danger of damage to healthy tissues. This laser surgery can be used to cure some types of epilepsy.

Vagus Nerve Stimulation

One technique used to treat epilepsy is vagus nerve stimulation. This involves implanting a small electrical device under the skin below the left collar bone. Wires from the device are wrapped around the person's vagus nerve in the neck in a small operation. The vagus nerve carries messages to and from major control centers in the brain. A neurologist can program the device to send impulses that try to prevent seizures. If a person senses a seizure coming on, they can activate the device to send extra messages to the brain to prevent it.

Robotic Devices

One day, it may be possible to implant devices that automatically sense when a seizure is about to happen. Scientists have already developed some miniature computerized "robotic" devices that, once inserted in the bloodstream, can detect the levels of various chemicals in the body. If such devices could sense the sudden, irregular surges of nerve impulses that trigger a seizure and send out counter-signals, a complete cure for epilepsy may be possible.

SEIZURE DOGS

There are dogs that can sense their owner's seizure about 30 seconds before it happens. It is not exactly understood how the dogs do this. It could be that they notice their owner behaving differently or sense an unusual body odor, electrical signals or other aura. The dogs are trained to bark, press against the person, or to sit down and not move to warn that a seizure is about to happen.

▶ *This six-year-old girl has inherited a form of epilepsy that randomly produces rapid jerks of her body lasting less than a second. Rooney, her dog, is a seizure dog, trained to alert her when she is about to have an attack.*

Glossary

absence seizure a seizure in which the person appears to be vacant or daydreaming for a few moments, used to be called a petit mal

acupuncture a technique developed in Chinese medicine that treats ailments and other problems by inserting special needles into specific places in the body

anti-epileptic drug (AED) a medicine or drug used to control the symptoms of epilepsy, also known as an anti-convulsant

aura a partial seizure that acts as a warning of a generalized seizure

complementary treatment treatment that helps, or works alongside, the main treatment. Often it is not known how effective a complementary medicine actually is

contract to become smaller or narrower

diabetes a condition where the body does not produce enough insulin, a hormone that breaks down sugar in the blood

diagnose to identify a condition or disease after careful examination of the body and symptoms

DNA short for deoxyribonucleic acid, a molecule that contains the genetic instructions for how a living being lives and grows

EEG a recording device known as an electroencephalogram. It records electrical activity in the brain.

epilepsy a condition of the brain involving irregular electrical activity that can result in seizures

generalized seizure a seizure that affects the whole brain from its onset and causes a person to lose consciousness

grand mal a term once used for tonic-clonic seizures

hormonal to do with hormones, substances produced by the body that regulate how various organs work

incision a small cut used in surgery

MRI a scan known as a magnetic resonance imaging device that uses the science of radiation to view the structure and function of the body.

nerves cells in the body that make up the nervous system, including the brain. Groups of neurons (brain cells) make up nerves

nervous system the network made up of nerves, the spinal column and the brain

neurologist a doctor who specializes in the health, conditions, diseases, and treatment of the brain

neurons scientific name for nerve cells. These communicate with one another and other parts of the body via electrical signals

partial seizure a type of seizure that affects only a part of the brain

petit mal a term once used for absence seizures

photochromic a clear glass that can darken when exposed to bright light

saliva a liquid made in the mouth

seizure any type of irregular electrical activity in the brain. An epileptic seizure causes a person to feel strange, uneasy, and maybe fall to the ground unconscious and twitch or jerk. It can last from a few seconds to several minutes

siblings brothers and sisters

side effects unwanted symptoms of any medical treatment

stroke the bursting of a blood vessel in the brain

symptoms changes in the body that can indicate that a disease or other condition is present

synapses narrow gaps in between neurons, across which neurons pass messages to each other using electrical signals

tonic-clonic seizure a severe type of seizure where a person loses consciousness and experiences convulsions, used to be called grand mal

trigger something that sets something else off; for example, flashing lights can trigger an epileptic seizure

tumor an abnormal mass of cells

vagus nerve a group of nerve fibers that carry signals to and from the brain, down through the neck, to the digestive system and heart. Many of the signals are related to the body's automatic actions

Further Information

Books

Epilepsy Explained: A Book for People Who Want to Know More
Markus Reuber, Oxford University Press, 2009

Epilepsy In Our Words: Personal Accounts of Living with Seizures
Edited by Steven C. Schachter, Oxford University Press, 2008

Epilepsy: Patient and Family Guide
Orrin Devinsky, Demos Medical Publishing, 2007

Epilepsy: The Ultimate Teen Guide (It Happened to Me)
Kathlyn Gay, The Scarecrow Press, 2007

Organizations

Antiepileptic Drug Pregnancy Registry
www.aedpregnancyregistry.org
1-888-AED-AED4

Center for Disease Control
www.cdc.gov/epilepsy

Charlie Foundation to Help Cure Pediatric Epilepsy
www.charliefoundation.org
1-800-FOR-KETO

Citizens United for Research in Epilepsy (CURE)
www.CUREepilepsy.org
(312)-255-1801

Epilepsy Foundation
www.epilepsyfoundation.org
1-800-EFA-1000

Epilepsy Institute
www.epilepsyinstitute.org
(212)-677-8550

Epilepsy Therapy Development Project
www.epilepsytdp.org
(703)-437-4250

Family Caregiver Alliance/ National Center on Caregiving
www.caregiver.org
1-800-445-8106

International RadioSurgery Association
www.irsa.org
(717)-260-9808

National Council on Patient Information and
Education
www.talkaboutrx.org
(301)-656-8565

National Family Caregivers Association
www.thefamilycaregiver.org
1-800-896-3650

National Organization for Rare Disorders (NORD)
www.rarediseases.org
1-800-999-NORD

People Against Childhood Epilepsy (PACE)
www.paceusa.org
(212)-665-PACE

Web Sites

Canadian Teens and Epilepsy:
What You Need to Know
www.epilepsy.ca/eng/content/teens.html

The International League Against Epilepsy (ILAE)
www.epilepsy.org

Epilepsy—Mayo Clinic
www.mayoclinic.com/health/epilepsy/DS00342

Epilepsy and Seizure Information
www.epilepsy.com

Note to Parents and Teachers: Every effort has been made by the publishers to ensure that these web sites are suitable for children, that they are of the highest educational value, and that they contain no inappropriate or offensive material. However, because of the nature of the Internet, it is impossible to guarantee that the contents of these sites will not be altered. We strongly advise that Internet access is supervised by a responsible adult.

Index

absence seizures 11, 17, 21
acupuncture 26, 27
alcohol 19
Alexander the Great 13
animals with epilepsy 31
anti-convulsants 24, 26
anti-epileptic drugs (AEDs) 24, 26, 27, 34, 37, 38
aromatherapy 26
atonic seizures 11, 16
auras 15, 29, 38

biofeedback 29
blood tests 20
Bonaparte, Napoleon 13
brain 8, 10-11, 14, 15, 16, 19, 20, 24, 25, 29, 36, 38
brain damage 11, 20, 24, 25, 32, 37, 38

Caesar, Julius 13
Carroll, Lewis 36
children 8
   brain development 8, 36
   medication 26, 29, 30, 32
   school 32-33
   seizures 13, 30, 31, 32, 33
complementary treatments 26-27
computers 11, 18, 20, 29, 32

diagnosis 20-21, 26
diet 19
discrimination 37
DNA 12

EEG scans 20, 21, 25, 29
elderly 8, 37
employment 28, 36, 37
epilepsy nurses 31, 32

families 30-31
Faneca, Alan 35
first aid 23

generalized seizures 11, 15, 16-17
genes 12
genetic causes of epilepsy 12-13
Glover, Danny 13
grand mal 11 *see also* tonic-clonic seizures

helmets 32, 34
Hippocrates 8
homeopathy 26
Horovitz, Adam 13

ID bracelets 28, 29
implants 38
inheritance 12-13

Kemp, Martin 13

laser surgery 38
Lenin, Vladimir 13
light sensitivity 18, 19, 30

Mayall, Rik 13
medi-alert bracelets 22, 28, 29
medication 15, 29, 31
   affect on threshold 19
   reducing or preventing seizures 24, 25, 28
   school 32
   side effects 25, 26, 37, 38
   taking 26-27
medicines 19, 24, 25, 26, 27, 29, 31, 32, 37
MRI scans 20, 25
myoclonic seizures 11, 16

nervous system 10-11, 20, 26
neurologists 15, 20, 21, 25, 27, 29, 31, 34, 38
neurons 10, 11, 25
partial seizures 11, 14-15
petit mal 11 *see also* absence seizures

recovery position 22

school 27, 29, 32-33
secondarily generalized seizures 11, 15
seizure dogs 38, 39
sports 28, 32, 34-35
status epilepticus 24
stress 18, 31
surgery 24, 25, 38
symptoms 8, 11, 12, 14, 15, 16, 17, 23, 35
synapses 10

tonic seizures 11
tonic-clonic seizures 11, 15, 16, 17, 22-23
triggers 13, 18-19, 20, 24, 30, 31, 32, 34, 35, 38
twins 12, 13

vagus nerve 10, 38

Titles and Contents in Explaining . . .

Explaining Asthma
What is Asthma? • History of Asthma • Increase in Asthma • Who has Asthma? • Healthy Lungs • How Asthma Affects the Lungs • What Triggers Asthma? • Asthma and Allergies • Diagnosing Asthma • Preventing an Attack • Relieving an Attack • What to Do During an Attack • Growing Up with Asthma • Living with Asthma • Asthma and Exercise • Asthma Treatments

Explaining Autism
What is Autism? • Autism: A Brief History • The Rise of Autism • The Autistic Spectrum • The Signs of Autism • Autism and Inheritance • The Triggers of Autism • Autism and the Body • Autism and Mental Health • Can Autism Be Treated? • Living with Autism • Autism and Families • Autism and School • Asperger Syndrome • Autism and Adulthood • The Future for Autism

Explaining Blindness
What is Blindness? • Causes and Effects • Visual Impairment • Color Blindness and Night Blindness • Eye Tests • Treatments and Cures • Coping with Blindness • Optical Aids • On the Move • Guide Dogs and Canes • Home Life • Blindness and Families • Blindness at School • Blindness as an Adult • Blindness, Sports, and Leisure • The Future for Blindness

Explaining Cerebral Palsy
What is Cerebral Palsy? • The Causes of Cerebral Palsy • Diagnosis • Types of Cerebral Palsy • Other Effects of Cerebral Palsy • Managing Cerebral Palsy • Other Support • Technological Support • Communication • How It Feels • Everyday Life • Being at School • Cerebral Palsy and the Family • Into Adulthood • Raising Awareness • The Future

Explaining Cystic Fibrosis
What is Cystic Fibrosis? • Cystic Fibrosis: A Brief History • What Causes Cystic Fibrosis? • Screening and Diagnosis • The Effects of Cystic Fibrosis • How is Cystic Fibrosis Managed? • Infections and Illness • A Special Diet • Clearing the Airways • Physical Exercise • Cystic Fibrosis and Families • Cystic Fibrosis at School • Growing Up with Cystic Fibrosis • New Treatments • The Future

Explaining Deafness
What is Deafness? • Ears and Sounds • Types of Deafness • Causes of Deafness • Signs of Deafness • Diagnosis • Treating Deafness • Lip Reading • Sign Language • Deafness and Education • Schools for the Deaf • Deafness and Adulthood • Technology • Deafness and the Family • Fighting Discrimination • The Future for Deafness

Explaining Diabetes
What is Diabetes? • Diabetes: A Brief History • Type 1 Diabetes • Type 2 Diabetes • Symptoms and Diagnosis • Medication • Hypoglycemia • Eyes, Skin, and Feet • Other Health Issues • Healthy Eating and Drinking • Physical Activity • Living with Diabetes • Diabetes and Families • Diabetes at School • Growing Up with Diabetes • Diabetes Treatment

Explaining Down Syndrome
What is Down Syndrome? • Changing Attitudes • Who has Down Syndrome? • What are Chromosomes? • The Extra Chromosome • Individual Differences • Health Problems • Testing for Down Syndrome • Diagnosing at Birth • Babies with Down Syndrome • Toddlers with Down Syndrome • At School • Friendships and Fun • Effects on the Family • Living Independently • The Future

Explaining Epilepsy
What is Epilepsy? • Causes and Effects • Who has Epilepsy? • Partial Seizures • Generalized Seizures • Triggers • Diagnosis • How You Can Help • Controlling Epilepsy • Taking Medicines • Living with Epilepsy • Epilepsy and Families • Epilepsy at School • Sports and Leisure • Growing Up with Epilepsy • Epilepsy Treatments

Explaining Food Allergies
What are Food Allergies? • Food Allergies: A Brief History • Food Aversion, Intolerance, or Allergy? • What Is an Allergic Reaction? • Food Allergies: Common Culprits • Anaphylaxis • Testing for Food Allergies • Avoiding Allergic Reactions • Treating Allergic Reactions • Food Allergies on the Rise • Food Allergies and Families • Food Allergies and Age • Living with Food Allergies • 21st Century Problems • Treatment for Food Allergies